MAP BASICS

All About ROAD MAPS AND GPS

By Barbara M. Linde

Gareth Stevens
PUBLISHING

Please visit our website, www.garethstevens.com. For a free color catalog of all our high-quality books, call toll free 1-800-542-2595 or fax 1-877-542-2596.

Cataloging-in-Publication Data
Names: Linde, Barbara M.
Title: All about road maps and GPS / Barbara M. Linde.
Description: New York : Gareth Stevens Publishing, 2019. | Series: Map basics | Includes glossary and index.
Identifiers: ISBN 9781538232682 (pbk.) | ISBN 9781538229194 (library bound) | ISBN 9781538232699 (6pack)
Subjects: LCSH: Roads–Maps–Juvenile literature. | Global Positioning System–Juvenile literature. | Map reading–Juvenile literature.
Classification: LCC GA130.L56 2019 | DDC 912.01'4–dc23

First Edition

Published in 2019 by
Gareth Stevens Publishing
111 East 14th Street, Suite 349
New York, NY 10003

Designer: Sarah Liddell
Editor: Monika Davies

Photo credits: Cover, p. 1 (map) robert cicchetti/Shutterstock.com; cover, p. 1 (GPS) Pincasso/Shutterstock.com; pp. 5, 9, 11, 13 Rainer Lesniewski/Shutterstock.com; p. 7 Kristi Blokhin/Shutterstock.com; p. 15 drosostalitsa/Shutterstock.com; p. 17 (main) Andrey Armyagov/Shutterstock.com; p. 17 (inset) CW craftsman/Shutterstock.com; p. 19 Rawpixel.com/Shutterstock.com.

Printed in the United States of America

CPSIA compliance information: Batch #CW19GS: For further information contact Gareth Stevens, New York, New York at 1-800-542-2595.

CONTENTS

What Is a Road Map? 4

What's on a Road Map? 6

Are We There Yet? 8

Which Way Are We Going? 10

How Do We Get There? 12

Neighborhood Maps 14

What Is GPS? 16

How Is GPS Used? 18

Map It! 20

Glossary 22

For More Information 23

Index 24

Words in the glossary appear in **bold** type the first time they are used in the text.

WHAT IS A ROAD MAP?

We go places all the time. Near or far, sometimes we might not know how to get where we're going. Road maps help guide us! Road maps show all kinds of roads. Some include natural features, such as bodies of water. They may also show the layout of a city or fun places to stop.

This road map of New York State shows all of its roadways, cities, and **boundaries** with other states and Canada. You could use this map to travel anywhere in the state!

JUST THE FACTS

A road map from over 1,500 years ago showed the roads of the Roman Empire from Spain to India. A copy of this map from the 13th century is over 22 feet (6.7 m) long!

NEW YORK STATE ROAD MAP

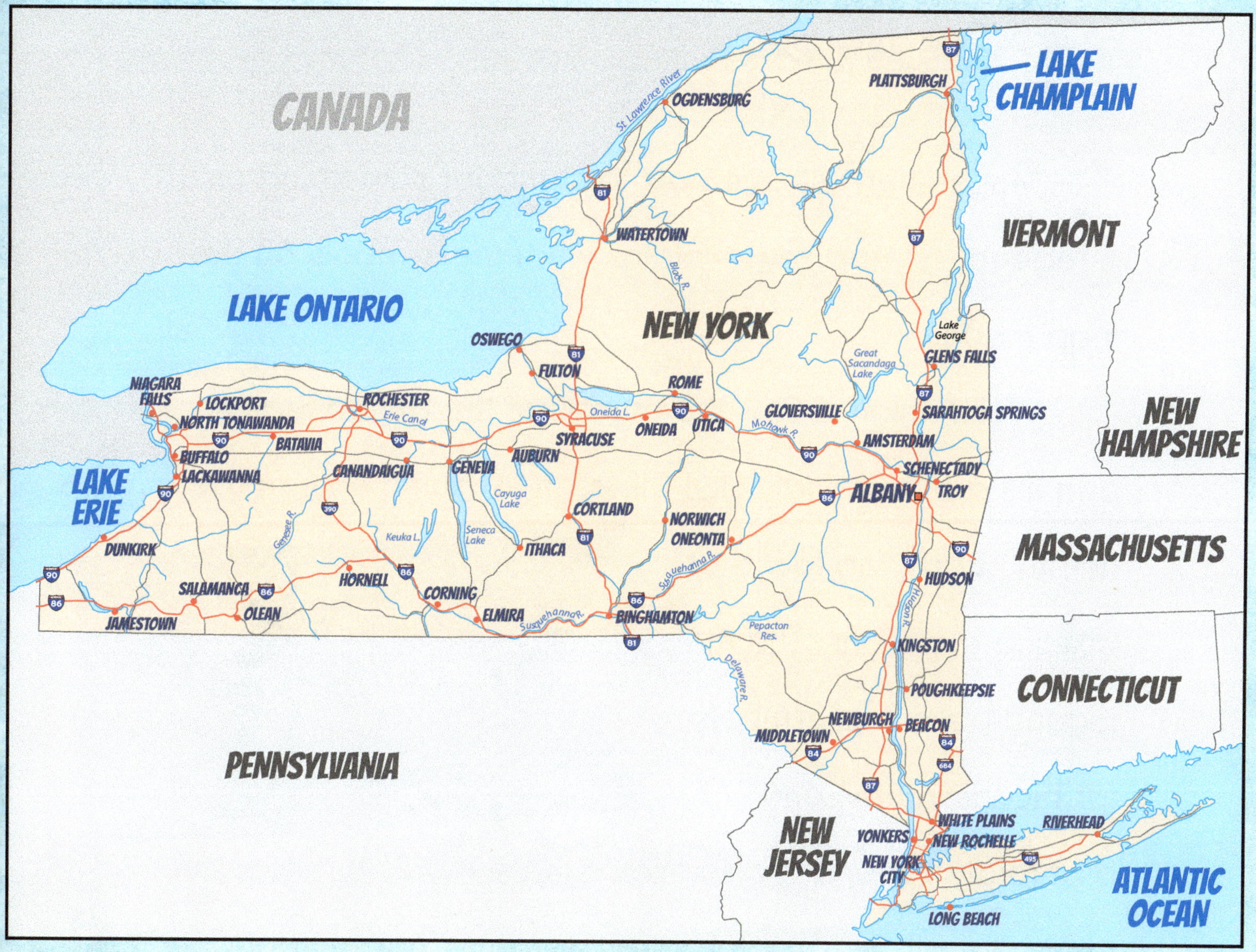

This road map shows the major highways that run through New York State, as well as bodies of water nearby, including Lake Ontario.

WHAT'S ON A ROAD MAP?

Maps often use **symbols** to stand for something else. A **legend**, or map key, explains what the symbols on the map mean.

Washington, DC, is the capital of the United States, and it's a bike-friendly city! Bikers in Washington can use a helpful road map found at bikeshare stations. The map's legend describes symbols for bicycle **routes** and bike-related shops. It also shows the symbols for stops on the Metrorail, Washington's train system. That's important to show since riders can take their bikes on the Metrorail.

JUST THE FACTS

People can rent bikes from several companies in Washington, DC. These types of companies are popping up all over. Is there one in your city yet?

There are around 270 Capital Bikeshare stations in Washington, DC. You can pick up a bike at a Capital Bikeshare location, ride it, and then return it to the station closest to you when you're done.

ARE WE THERE YET?

Road maps use a scale to show **distances**. This is helpful because maps show areas of land as much smaller than they actually are. An inch on the scale may stand for a certain distance in feet or miles on the map.

On this map of Arizona, the scale says 0.75 inches (1.9 cm) equals 50 miles (80.5 km). The cities of Phoenix and Tucson are about 1.5 inches (3.8 cm) apart. How far apart does that make the two cities in miles?

JUST THE FACTS

This road map also shows Arizona's bodies of water, including the Colorado River.

ARIZONA ROAD MAP

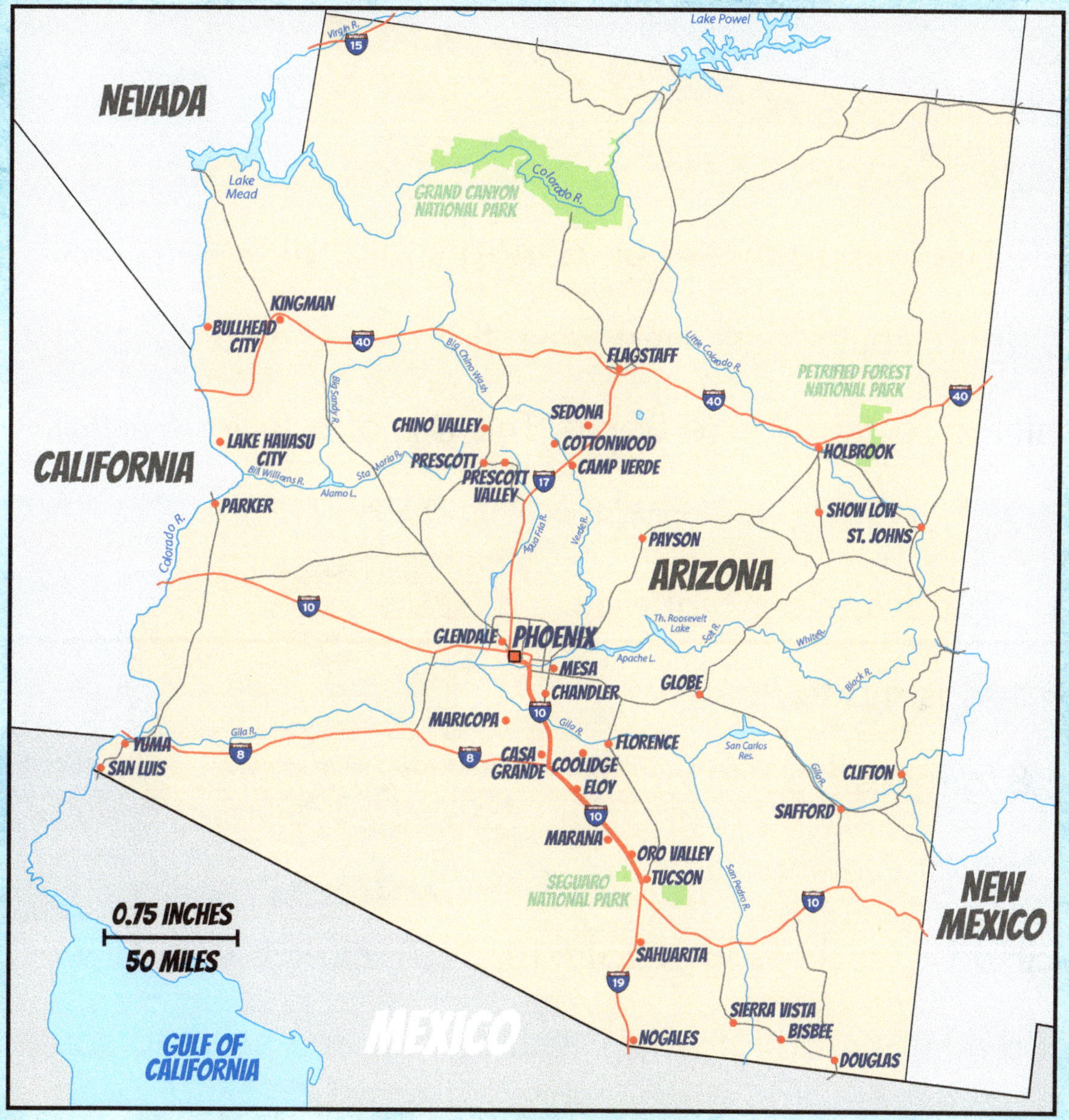

If you drive down Route 10 from Phoenix to Tucson, the actual trip would be about 113 miles (182 km).

WHICH WAY ARE WE GOING?

The compass rose on a map shows directions, such as north, south, east, and west. It can help you figure out which direction you're going. The top of a map is usually north, but check the compass rose to be sure.

The interstate highway system is made up of 46,876 miles (75,540 km) of roads! Even-numbered highways, such as Interstate 10 (I-10), stretch east to west. Odd-numbered highways, such as I-95, run north to south.

JUST THE FACTS

The longest interstate highway in the United States is I-90, which stretches more than 3,000 miles (4,828 km) between Boston, Massachusetts, and Seattle, Washington.

US INTERSTATE HIGHWAYS

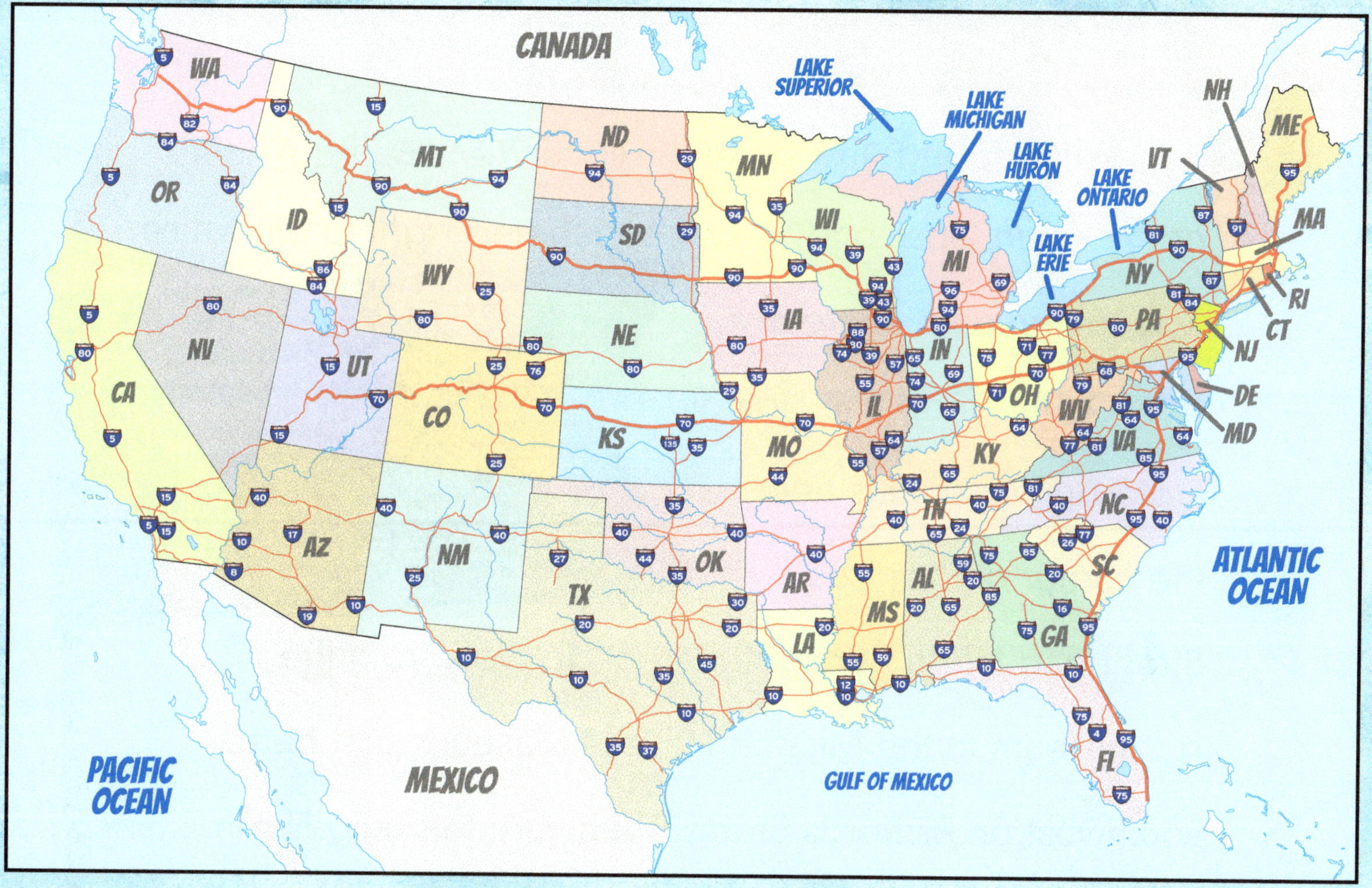

I-95 goes through 16 different states, which is the most of any interstate highway!

HOW DO WE GET THERE?

When giving and reading directions, use the words *north, south, east,* and *west.* Use *left* and *right* to tell which way to turn onto a street.

JUST THE FACTS

You might hear *uptown* and *downtown* when talking about a big city. *Downtown* usually refers to the business center of a city, while *uptown* refers to where people live.

On this map, the Hawaii State Art Museum is near the corner of Richards Street and North Beretania Street. To walk from the art museum to the Mission Houses Museum, first head southwest on Richards Street. Then, turn left onto North King Street. Keep walking until you see the Mission Houses Museum on your right, just after Punch Bowl Street.

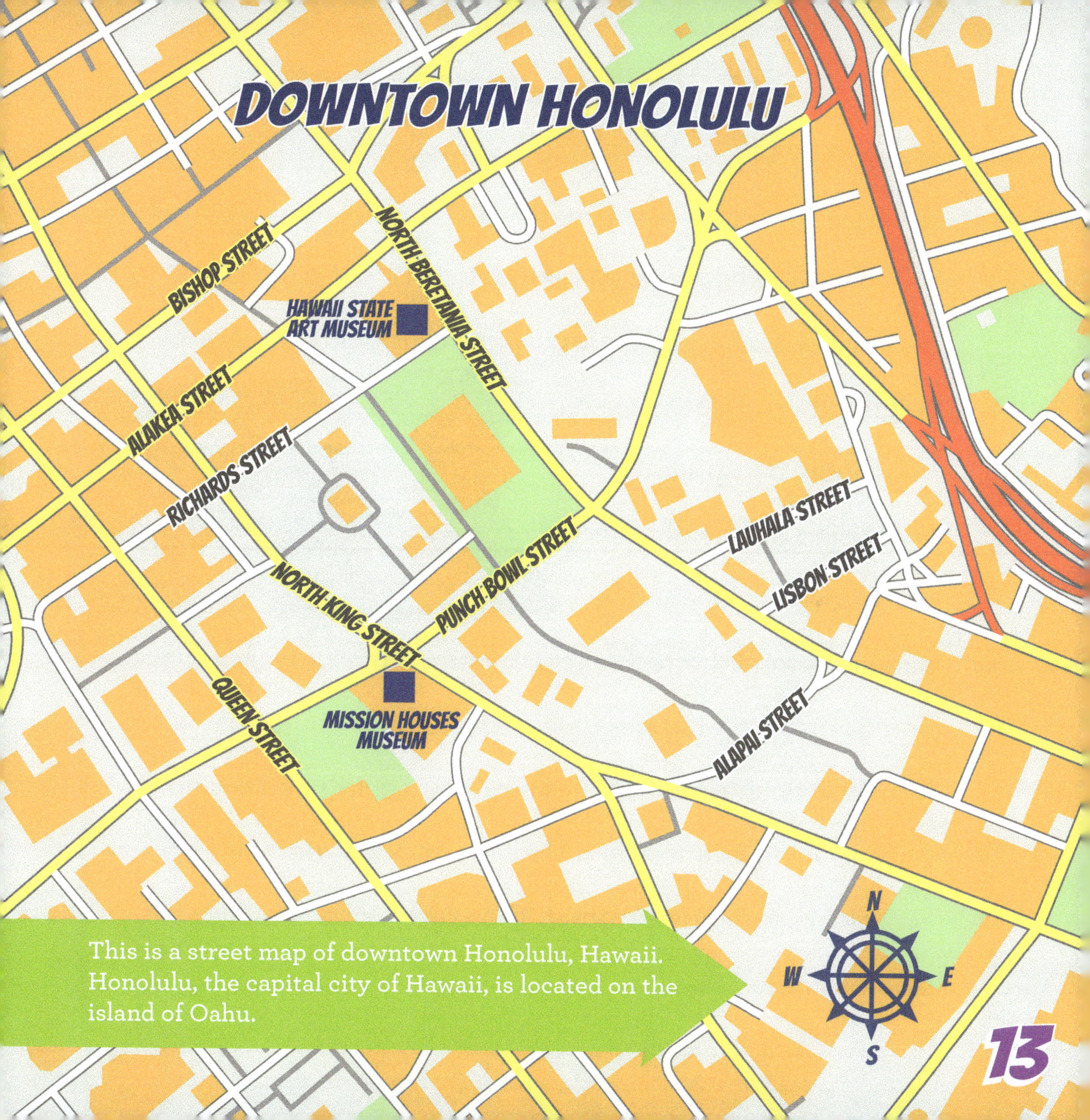

This is a street map of downtown Honolulu, Hawaii. Honolulu, the capital city of Hawaii, is located on the island of Oahu.

NEIGHBORHOOD MAPS

Neighborhood maps give details about a section of a city or town. These maps show roads and important neighborhood features such as schools and parks.

Using this neighborhood map, how would you give directions from the red house on the corner of Pine Avenue and Cherry Street to the blue house on the corner of Maple Avenue and Apple Street? You could say, "Go north on Pine Avenue. Then, turn right on Apple Street, and go two blocks to Maple Avenue. The blue house is on the left side of Apple Street."

JUST THE FACTS

In the United States, Second Street is a more popular road name than First Street!

NEIGHBORHOOD MAP

On this map, "streets" go in one direction, such as east to west, while "avenues" go in the opposite direction, such as north to south. This is the way some real-life cities have named their roads.

WHAT IS GPS?

The Global Positioning System (GPS) is owned by the United States government. It was created and is run by the US Air Force.

GPS is made of a group of 24 **satellites** that **orbit** Earth. These satellites send radio **signals** back to Earth all day, every day. The radio signals contain information that help pinpoint the exact location of someone or something.

JUST THE FACTS

When the first satellite for GPS was launched, only the military was allowed to use the system. It wasn't until 1983 that a form of GPS was available for public use.

Devices called receivers pick up these radio signals. Receivers are built into smartphones, as well as **navigation** systems in cars and airplanes.

GPS receivers use information from three to four satellites to locate someone's exact position on Earth.

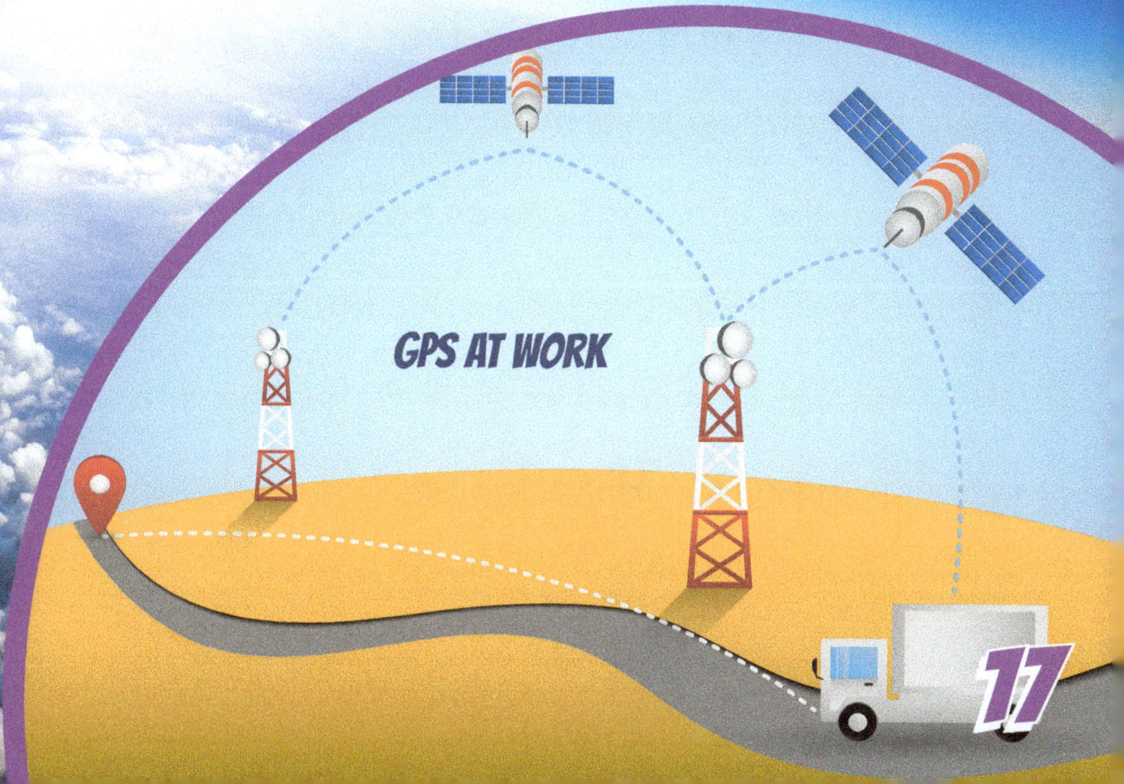

HOW IS GPS USED?

Using GPS is like using a paperless road map. You can enter the address where you want to go into your smartphone or car navigation system. Both have a GPS receiver built in. The GPS receiver knows exactly where you are, which helps the navigation system figure out the different routes you can take.

JUST THE FACTS

GPS gives you step-by-step directions to let you know exactly how far to go on each street and where to turn.

GPS helps plan your route. The route then shows up on your device's screen. Sometimes, a voice will give you step-by-step directions to your destination.

GPS can be used for more than just walking and driving. It can also help hikers, kayakers, bikers, and others plan their travel route.

MAP IT!

How well do you know your neighborhood? Learn more about where you live by making a neighborhood map! Work with an adult or a friend who lives near you.

When creating your map, be sure to include the houses, parks, bodies of water, shopping centers, and community buildings in your neighborhood.

After you've finished your map, use direction words to describe to your classmates how to get around your neighborhood. Just for fun, try to sound like the voice on a GPS!

MAP YOUR NEIGHBORHOOD!

1. WALK AROUND YOUR NEIGHBORHOOD. USE A **COMPASS** AND MARK THE DIRECTION (*NORTH, SOUTH, EAST*, OR *WEST*) YOU'RE WALKING ON A SHEET OF PAPER.

2. DRAW YOUR NEIGHBORHOOD MAP AS YOU GO. LABEL THE ROADS YOU WALK DOWN WITH THEIR NAMES.

3. CREATE SYMBOLS FOR DIFFERENT BUILDINGS IN YOUR AREA. ADD A LEGEND TO YOUR MAP THAT SAYS WHAT EACH SYMBOL STANDS FOR.

4. DRAW A FINAL COPY OF YOUR MAP ON PAPER. DON'T FORGET TO ADD A COMPASS ROSE!

GLOSSARY

boundary: something that marks the limit of an area or a place

compass: a tool for finding directions by using a magnetic needle

device: a tool or machine made to perform a task

distance: the amount of space between two places or things

legend: a list that explains the symbols on a map

navigation: the science of plotting and following a path from one place to another

orbit: to travel in a circle or oval around something

route: a course that people travel

satellite: an object that circles Earth in order to collect and send information or aid in communication

signal: a message, sound, or image that is carried by waves of light or sound

symbol: a picture, shape, or object that stands for something else

FOR MORE INFORMATION

BOOKS

Derrick, Martin. *North American Road Trips: Unforgettable Journeys of a Lifetime*. New York, NY: Chartwell Books, 2018.

Fullman, Joe. *My Family Travel Map: North America*. New York, NY: Lonely Planet Kids, 2018.

Rand McNally. *Kids' Road Atlas*. Chicago, IL: Rand McNally, 2016.

WEBSITES

How Does GPS Work?
spaceplace.nasa.gov/gps-pizza/en
Learn how GPS works by watching a short video by NASA.

Printable Maps
climate.gov/maps-data/data-snapshots/start
Visit this website to view road maps of the United States or individual states!

Publisher's note to educators and parents: Our editors have carefully reviewed these websites to ensure that they are suitable for students. Many websites change frequently, however, and we cannot guarantee that a site's future contents will continue to meet our high standards of quality and educational value. Be advised that students should be closely supervised whenever they access the internet.

INDEX

Arizona 8, 9

avenues 15

bicycles 6, 7

bodies of water 4, 5, 8, 20

cities 4, 6, 12, 14

compass 21

compass rose 10, 21

directions 10, 12, 14, 15, 18, 20

Global Positioning System (GPS) 16, 17, 18, 19, 20

highways 5, 10, 11

Honolulu 13

legend 6, 21

navigation systems 16, 18

neighborhood maps 14, 15, 20, 21

New York State 4, 5

radio signals 16

receivers 16, 17, 18

roads 4, 10, 14, 15, 21

Roman Empire 4

satellites 16, 17

scale 8

smartphones 16, 18

streets 12, 14, 15, 18

symbols 6, 21

US Air Force 16

Washington, DC 6, 7